Peter

THE FISHERMAN

The Story of Peter
accurately retold from the Bible
ım Matthew, Mark, Luke and John), by
CARINE MACKENZIE

Design and Illustrations
Mackay Design Associates Ltd

Published in Great Britain by
CHRISTIAN FOCUS PUBLICATIONS LTD
Geanies House, Fearn, Tain, Ross-shire IV20 1TW, Scotland
http://www.christianfocus.com
© 1980 Christian Focus Publications Ltd ISBN 0 906731 08 9
B/G 3-8

Reprint 1984
New edition 1988.
Reprinted 1992
Reprinted 1998

Long ago, in the town of Capernaum by the Lake of Galilee, lived a man called Simon and his family. Simon and his brother Andrew were fishermen.

One day Andrew met Jesus and he knew that He was Christ, the Saviour of sinners, whom God had promised to send. Andrew hurried to tell Simon the good news and then he took Simon to see Jesus.

Jesus spoke kindly to Simon and gave him another name. He called him Peter, which means "a stone".

I am sure that Simon Peter would often think afterwards of that wonderful day when he met Jesus.

One night, Simon Peter and Andrew went fishing with James and John. They fished all night but caught nothing.

In the morning they took their boats
to the shore and began to wash
their fishing nets.

Then they noticed Jesus standing at
the shore. There were many people
with Him, crowding round Him to
hear the wonderful things He was
saying about God.

Jesus came and stepped into
Peter's boat and asked him to push
out from the land. Then Jesus sat
down and preached to the people
from the boat.

When Jesus finished speaking to the people He said to Peter, "Go out to deeper water and let down your nets to catch fish."

Peter answered, "Master, we have been busy all night long, and have not caught any fish. But we will do as You say."

How surprised Peter was when he and Andrew tried to pull in their net. It was so full of fish that it began to break.

James and John came to help them and they all pulled together with all their might. Soon both boats were filled with so much fish that they were almost sinking.

What marvellous power Jesus had over the creatures of the sea!

When Peter saw the great power of Jesus he fell down on his knees in front of Him. "Keep away from me, O Lord," he said to Jesus, "for I am a sinful man."

Peter knew that he had a sinful heart and that he had done many wrong things in his life. He realised too that Jesus was God and that He had no sin in Him at all.

Jesus said to Peter, "Do not be afraid. From now on you will work for me." Jesus chose Peter to be one of His special helpers, called disciples, and so He told Peter to follow Him.

Jesus told Andrew, James and John also to follow Him.

When Peter and Andrew, James and John, brought their boats back to the shore they gave up their fishing business and followed Jesus. Jesus called them "fishers of men" because their new work was to bring men to Jesus the Saviour.

One Sabbath day Peter went to the synagogue in Capernaum. Jesus was preaching that day. After the service, Peter invited Jesus to his house.

In the house, Peter's wife's mother was very ill in bed, with a bad fever. The family was very worried.

"Can You do anything to help her?" they asked Jesus.

Jesus went to her bedside and touched her hand. She became better right away. The fever was completely gone and she felt quite cool.

She felt so well that she got up at once to give food to Jesus and Peter and the others.

So Peter again saw Jesus' wonderful power: this time, His power over sickness.

Not long afterwards Peter saw
Jesus' power in yet another way.
Jesus and the disciples set out to
sail over to the other side of the
lake.

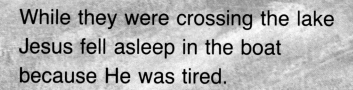

While they were crossing the lake
Jesus fell asleep in the boat
because He was tired.

Soon a great storm blew up. The
wind howled. The waves came right
over the sides of the boat.

The disciples became more and
more frightened even although
Jesus was in the boat with them.

Then they wakened Him up. "Lord,
save us," they shouted, "we are
going to drown!"

Jesus said to them, "Why are you
so afraid? How weak your faith is."

Jesus then spoke to the wind and to
the sea and said, "Peace, be still."

The wind stopped blowing. The sea
became very calm.

The disciples were astonished.
Jesus had power over the wind and
sea too.

One evening, after a busy day at the other side of the lake, Peter and the other disciples were told by Jesus to sail back across the lake.

Jesus did not go with them. He wanted to be alone for a time to pray to God His Father.

As the disciples were rowing across the lake, it became dark. The wind was blowing strongly against them and the lake was very rough and stormy. The little boat was tossed about by the waves.

Then out of the darkness the disciples saw someone walking on the waves. They were all terrified. "It's a ghost!" one of them said.

But then they heard the voice of Jesus, which they all knew and loved, saying, "It is I. Do not be afraid."

Peter shouted back, "Lord, if it is really You, tell me to walk on the water to meet You".

"Come," Jesus replied.

So Peter climbed over the side of the boat and began to walk on the water towards Jesus. The wind was still blowing hard. Peter looked at the tossing waves and he became afraid. Then he began to sink!

He shouted to Jesus in fear, "Lord, save me!" Jesus reached out His hand and caught hold of Peter.

"Why did you doubt?" He asked Peter.

They went back into the boat and the wind died down immediately.

The other disciples were amazed by
what they had seen. They
worshipped Jesus and were sure
that He was indeed the Son of God.

Peter and the other disciples went along with Jesus each day, as He travelled from town to town and around the country, preaching to the people.

One day in Caesarea Philippi, Jesus asked His disciples, "Who do people say I am?"

"Some say You are John the Baptist," they answered, "and some say Elijah, and some say Jeremiah or one of the prophets."

"And who do *you* say I am?" Jesus asked them.

Peter was first to reply. "You are Christ, the Son of the living God," he said.

Peter was right and Jesus said to him, "It is my Father in heaven who has taught you that".

What would your answer be if Jesus were to ask you the question, "Who do you say I am?"

Just as God taught Peter to give the right answer, so He can teach you.

One day, in Capernaum, Peter saw the temple money collectors coming up to him.

They asked him, "Does your Master pay money for the work of the temple?" "Yes," said Peter.

Peter went to tell Jesus about the money collectors. When they met, Jesus spoke first, for He knew what Peter was going to say.

"What do you think?" Jesus asked Peter. "Would a king take tax money from his own children or from strangers?"

"From strangers," replied Peter.

Jesus said to him, "Then the children are free."

Jesus meant that He was the Son of God and did not need to pay money for His Father's house, the temple. But He did not want to offend anyone and so He said He would pay the money.

Where would they get the money from?

Jesus told Peter, "Go down to the shore and throw a fishing hook into the sea and take up the first fish that you catch. When you open its mouth you will find a coin which will pay the temple money for us both."

Peter believed in Jesus' power over all things and he did just as Jesus had told him.

Peter continued following Jesus but some people followed Jesus for a short time only. They did not truly love Him. When things became difficult, they left Him.

One day Jesus said to the twelve disciples, "Will you go away and leave me too?"

Again, Peter was the first one to answer. "Lord, to whom shall we go? You have the words of eternal life. We believe and are sure that You are Christ, the Son of the living God".

By this answer, Peter showed his faith in Jesus Christ.

He also showed that he loved Jesus more than he loved anyone else by working for Jesus, as a "fisher of men," to the end of his days.

We hope to tell you more stories about Peter in the next book, called, 'Peter, The Disciple'.